Back to School
with Pepper
the Pointer

Written by Kyrsten Amanto

Illustrated by QBN Studios

Back to School
with **Pepper**
the Pointer

Copyright © 2023 by Kyrsten Amanto

Illustrated by QBN Studios

To my **students**, past, present, and future...
You can do hard things.

To my **family**... thanks for reminding me that I can too.

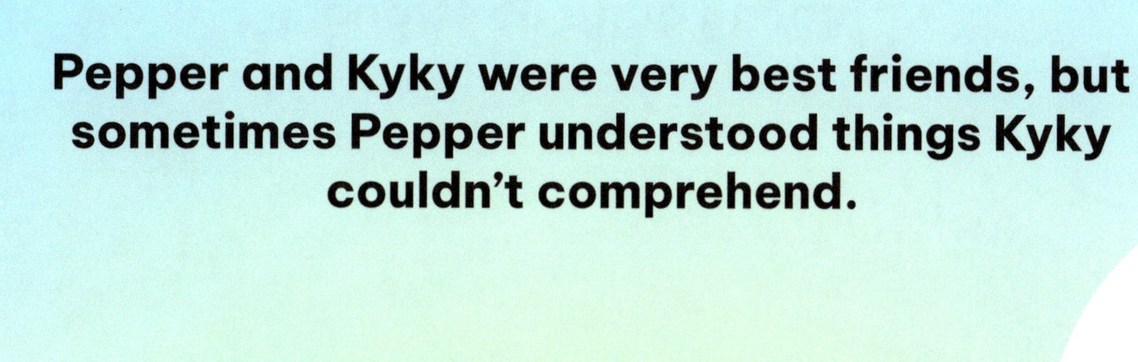

Pepper and Kyky were very best friends, but sometimes Pepper understood things Kyky couldn't comprehend.

Like when the sun didn't hang around quite as long and the song of the cicadas didn't sound quite as strong...

Pepper knew their fun summer was coming to an end, and soon she'd have a very upset best friend.

Kyky was starting to lose her cool. Her nerves fluttered like butterflies around the word

OO L

What if her teacher had the voice of a witch, teeth like a mule, and was just plain cruel?

The thought made Kyky's eye start to twitch. Her voice began to change, it went up a high pitch!

That's final! That's it! I'm not going to school. I'd rather be covered in your stinky, hot drool!

Arms crossed and cheeks blushing, she stomped up to her room.
Pepper's tail barely made it before the door slammed...

There they sat together, feet and front paws dangling off the bed, as thoughts of supplies and classes flooded Kyky's head.

She mumbled distastefully about algebra, division, fractions, and equations. Pepper could sense Kyky was nervous about all these calculations.

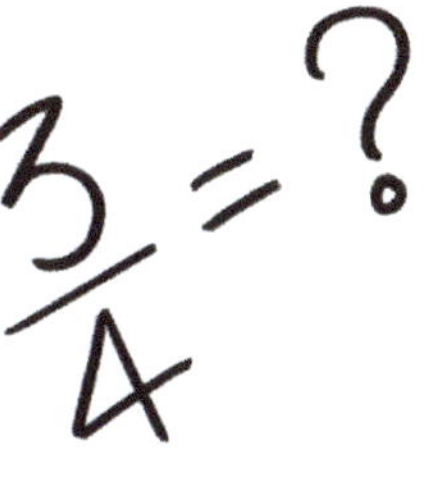

$50\sqrt{000000}$
$\dfrac{3}{4} = ?$
$y = mx + b$
$e = mc^2 (3.14)$
$+ 6.5 \div 2 \times 1$

That's final!
That's it!
I don't want to do math.
It sounds about as fun as
giving you a bath!

Pepper placed her gray and black chin atop her best friend's thighs. Kyky took a deep breath and released it as she closed her eyes.

For a moment a blanket of calm laid over the pair,
but then language arts concepts had Kyky pulling
at her hair!

There's rhyming, syllables, consonants, and tapping to blend. Digraphs, vowels, vocabulary, where does it end?!

"That's final!
That's it!
There's so much learning to do!"

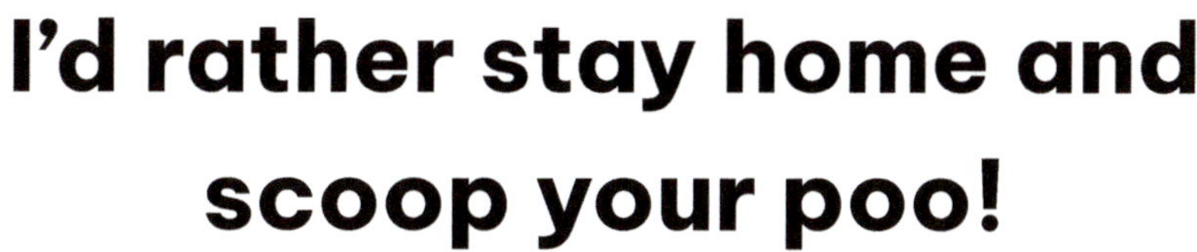

I'd rather stay home and
scoop your poo!

I don't even want to hear
about gym,
technology,
music,
and art...

"I'd rather sit here and listen to you fart!"

Kyky continued
to pace all
over the place
with her canine
pal just a step
behind.

Pepper heard whining,
complaining; any excuse
to avoid leaving home Kyky
could find.

Her mind was running wild, like Pepper after birds in the yard. It seemed like something more was bothering Kyky than school being hard.

The mental list of worries and things she was unsure of grew and grew, but one thing she knew...

"I'll just really miss you."

Pepper's ears perked up. She began sniffing and pointing all over the house...

...at a backpack,

sharp pencils,

and a clean white blouse.

She picked up a notebook and dropped
it at Kyky's feet. With a pat and a
smile, she was rewarded with a treat.

Okay, okay… so maybe there's no need to fret. Math and numbers may be really tough, and special classes will probably have some confusing stuff. Reading and writing will be a challenge, I bet, but it's not that I can't do it, I just can't do it yet.

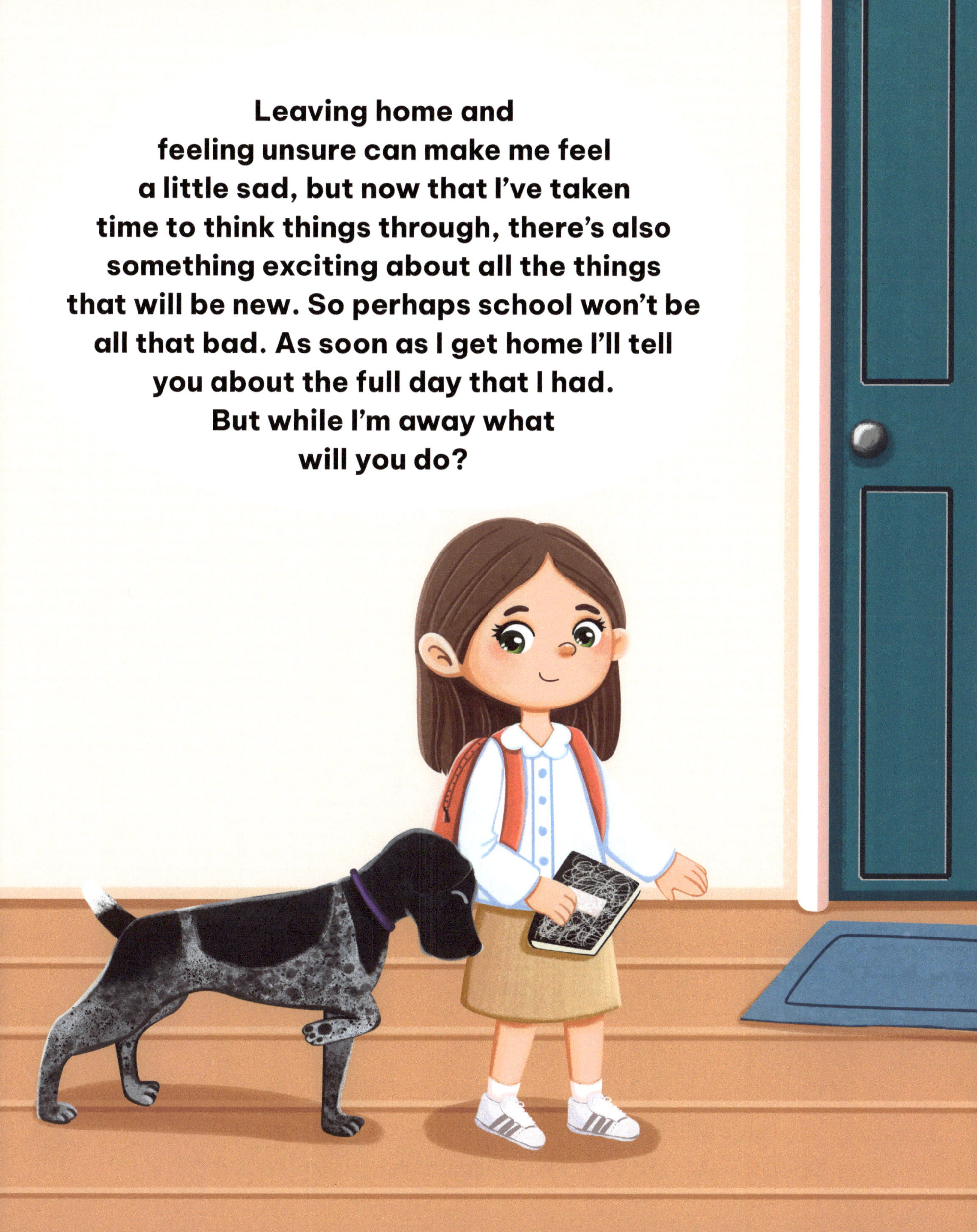

Leaving home and
feeling unsure can make me feel
a little sad, but now that I've taken
time to think things through, there's also
something exciting about all the things
that will be new. So perhaps school won't be
all that bad. As soon as I get home I'll tell
you about the full day that I had.
But while I'm away what
will you do?

I will stay here and wait for you
to tell me about the day and how you grew.

Author/Contributor Bio:

Kyrsten Amanto, a Pennsylvania born and bred educator, is not your typical dog-loving kindergarten teacher. She is also a children's book author, captivating young readers and listeners with relatable tales. What sets Kyrsten's stories apart is her intelligent, loyal German Shorthaired Pointer, Pepper, who takes center stage. Pepper, her canine companion, serves as a guiding light, using her natural pointing instincts to help young readers navigate through valuable life lessons.

Aside from Kyrsten's Bachelor's Degree in English and Master's Degree in Early Childhood Education, having spent countless hours in various classrooms and conversations with children lends itself to her understanding the importance of creating relatable, entertaining places for children to embark on a lesson of self discovery through reading.